Nineteenth Century America

THE

UNIONS

UNION SLOGANS

Nineteenth Century America

THE
UNIONS

written and illustrated by
LEONARD EVERETT FISHER

Holiday House · New York

Library of Congress Cataloging in Publication Data

Fisher, Leonard Everett.
  The unions.

  (Nineteenth century America)
  Includes index.
  Summary: Traces the growth and development of the
labor movement during the nineteenth century.
  1. Trade-unions—United States—History—Juvenile
literature. [1. Labor unions] I. Title. II. Series.
HD6508.F46   331.88'0973   81-6632
ISBN 0-8234-0434-X   AACR2

List of Illustrations

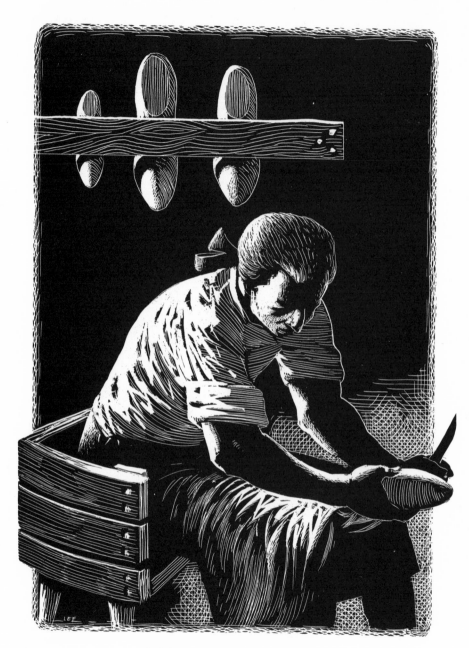

A COLONIAL SHOEMAKER

I. FIRST YEARS: 1630-1800

In 1633, the Massachusetts General Court decreed that colonial Boston shoemakers—there were not too many of them—could not charge prices other than those fixed by the court. The people of Boston complained that their shoes cost too much. They sought the protection of the court which represented the Crown, the British home government.

For the next fifteen years, Thomas Beard, Massachusetts' first shoemaking craftsman, and fellow shoemakers, protested the Crown's interference in the conduct of their trade. During this time, they petitioned the court for the right to organize themselves into a guild. They wanted to protect their interests and improve their lot in life. They knew they could not do all of this as individuals. They knew, too, that the colonial government would not help them as individuals either.

In 1648, the Crown gave in. It was unable to resist the years of clamor. The Massachusetts General Court granted a charter to the Boston shoemakers. They were permitted to form a "Company of Shoomakers." The guild was not a union in the modern sense. It had no real power to bargain or even win arguments with the authorities. Yet, it could petition the government without fear of arrest and hope that the court would at least listen to its complaints. This was the first time in

America that working craftsmen who labored from sunup to sundown could band together to discuss their common interests and be represented before the authorities by a common spokesman.

Colonial American craftsmen soon sensed a vague strength in their unity. Between 1659 and 1663, a rash of protests staged by working people swept the towns and hamlets of Massachusetts and Virginia. The complaints, for the most part, dealt with long hours of toil, low wages, and miserable working conditions.

During the 1700's, the American colonies grew so rapidly that the colonists often could not supply the goods they needed. Craftsmen—upholsterers, tanners, papermakers, and the like—who made their product by hand sometimes could not work fast enough to fill the demand.

England squeezed her colonies further. She passed laws limiting the quantity of goods made in the colonies —even hats! She increased the costs of raw materials needed to make most products and tried to regulate the selling price of everything. Finally, England tried to prohibit the colonists from trading with anyone but herself.

Unable to raise prices as they saw fit, mastercraftsmen—the employers—reduced the wages of their journeymen and apprentices—their employees. Although the employers were thus able to maintain a profit, their employees could not now afford to buy the very products they made. An uneasiness settled over the average colonial American working man and woman.

Bakers, printers, shoemakers and others organized "societies" and "turned out," or struck, the various workshops that employed them. They wanted shorter hours, higher wages, and better working conditions. They marched in picket lines, or "tramping committees," to protest. These strikes did not last very long. Usually, employers quickly agreed to the demands of the strikers. Once the demands were met, the strikers disbanded their societies. Without an organized society, the workers were no longer a threat to their employers. Knowing this, the employers quickly refused to honor the new agreements. Sometimes the workers struck the same employer over and over again. And just as often, the employers retracted the agreements. At other times, the employees, having struck once without much success, never tried again. Whatever the case, nothing seemed to change very much.

During the Revolutionary War (1775-1781), a fragile truce seemed to exist between American employers and their employees. Everyone was too busy fighting the British. Once England was defeated, free Americans who worked for a wage once more turned their attention to a better life for themselves and their families.

New York City printers formed a society in 1786 and went on strike. They demanded $1 a day for their work. Their employers granted the demand. The society disbanded having achieved its goal. But the employers did not renege on the deal. They honored the agreement made with their employees. Following the example set by the printing trade, others struck for higher wages—weavers, gunsmiths, wheelwrights and others. They all achieved their goal—pay raises. However, much of this was only temporary. Another day would come when another pay hike would be needed for the worker to stay even with the growing American economy.

In 1792, the Journeymen Cordwainers of Philadelphia [a cordwainer was a shoemaker] formed America's first permanent society, or union, and struck for higher wages, shorter hours, and better working conditions in 1799. What the shoemakers really wanted was a ten-hour workday, not the customary grind of eleven-or-twelve-hour workdays—Saturdays included. And this they wanted without a reduction in pay.

The strike went on for ten weeks. It was the longest turnout that had ever been staged in America. No shoes were made in Philadelphia during the strike. In the end, the shoemakers won an uneasy victory. They won their ten-hour day. But their employers would seek revenge in the courts seven years later.

Meanwhile the ten-hour workday, six-day work week of the Philadelphia shoemakers became the immediate goal for most American wage earners as the 19th century began. In time, the goal would change to an eight-hour workday, five-and-a-half-day work week.

Whatever the goal, the American labor movement had begun. Bitter, bloody struggles would mark its progress.

TURNOUT FOR A TEN-HOUR WORKDAY

II. CHANGING SYSTEMS: 1800-1825

With the invention of the steam engine by James Watt, and the water-powered, belt-driven spinning wheel by Sir Richard Arkwright, both in England in 1769, the Industrial Revolution became a force to be reckoned with. In less than fifty years following these inventions, startling changes in nearly every aspect of life would be unleashed upon an unsuspecting world. What had once been a predominantly agricultural society would now become a predominantly industrial society. Transportation, communication, fashion, farming, education, mining, construction, manufacturing, and more would never be the same again. In fact, for better or worse, nothing would ever be the same again.

The slow, quiet world of farmers, craftsmen, merchants and aristocrats of the 18th century—an orderly world in which everything and everyone seemed to have his or her place in life—was dissolving. It was being replaced by a noisy 19th century world of coal, smoke, steam, speed, and clacking machinery. Here the skilled and unskilled began to live in more congested squalor than anyone had dreamed of, laboring long hours on machines they did not own; using or toiling for the raw materials they could not own; producing a part of a product they would probably never own. And here

12

people labored for wages that barely paid the rent, hardly clothed them, and poorly fed them. It was a different world, a changing world, a world in which no one was quite sure where he or she was going.

The future seemed to belong not to the aristocrats and landed nobility, but to those who owned the machines, the factories, and the raw materials, not to mention the products made in these factories. To the average worker, the world was now being divided into two parts: rich employers who lived very well and poor employees who had no life at all except bone-weary hard labor.

By 1800, in America as elsewhere, some craftsmen who only knew how to make a product from start to finish by themselves using hand tools were slowly becoming old fashioned. Division of labor—dividing the work into simple steps to make a single product so that no one person made the product alone—was becoming the permanent way of manufacturing. The artisan whose training and singular abilities found expression in his own workshop was being replaced by a factory. The first such successful factory in America was the Almy, Brown and Slater cotton-spinning mill in Rhode Island, founded in 1790.

Where formerly it took one person to make one product—a hat, a shoe, a bolt of cloth—it now took several persons less time to make the same hat, the same shoe, the same bolt of cloth. Instead of using hand tools to make a shoe, for example, children, who could

FACTORY CHILDREN

not make a shoe by themselves, now worked at machines that made the shoe step by step. It was a faster,
cheaper method of providing the burgeoning American
marketplaces with the goods they needed and demanded. Moreover, the new system provided much-
needed jobs for an American population that would
nearly double in the twenty-year period 1790-1810*;
and increase fourteen times over between 1800-1900†.
The structure of production was being redesigned to
absorb and employ such a fast-developing mass of
people.

While inventor Eli Whitney was busy manufacturing
rifles in his Connecticut factory in 1804, the same
Philadelphia shoemakers who had struck for and had
won a ten-hour workday were busy planning new
moves against their employers. They had reorganized
themselves under a new name. Now they were the
"Federal Society of Journeymen Cordwainers." Like most
trade associations of the day, they kept their membership
roles secret. For one thing, they did not want their
members constantly bullied by employers. Also, not all
workers belonged to a society, so secrecy made it difficult
for employers to identify the source of any trouble.

By the same token, many workers often did not know

---

*U.S. population 1790: 3,929,000
                  1810: 7,224,000
†U.S. population 1800: 5,297,000
                  1900: 76,094,000
United States Department of Commerce, Bureau of the Census figures.

who employed them. The owners of the factories remained absent and anonymous, preferring to have managers run their businesses for them.

In 1806, eight members of the Federal Society of Journeymen Cordwainers were found out and arrested in Philadelphia. They were indicted on a charge of "criminal conspiracy." The crime they were accused of was organizing themselves into a "union" to force their employers into giving them pay raises. They were tried, found guilty by a jury of employers, and jailed. The general public was unsympathetic to their cause, including those who worked for a day's pay. The convicted shoemakers were considered unpatriotic troublemakers and worse—agents of foreign governments. No amount of appeal could reverse the decision.

For the next generation of Americans, it became illegal to organize a "union" or "club" whose members "conspired" to improve their wages. And anyone found to be a member of such an illegal organization was deemed to be a criminal, liable to arrest and prosecution for conspiracy. The same laws existed in England where industrialization was a few years ahead of the United States.

The 1806 decision that made trade unions illegal in America did not stop the various trades—printers, shoemakers, joiners, stonemasons, tailors, shipwrights, etc.—from secretly organizing and sometimes striking. The risks were great. But the alternative of poverty was worse. Many strikers were beaten by thugs hired by employers who thought they could club their employees into submission. Those who did not strike were called "scabs." Usually, they did not belong to the striking union. Few of the scabs escaped the fists and clubs of the strikers. Many of those who struck and were beaten for their trouble were hauled off to jail or simply fired.

With American independence hardly twenty-five years old, it was not surprising that large sections of the population nervously saw the so-called "conspiracy" of organized labor as "foreign" plots threatening the security of the United States. Despite the dangers, the illegality of their situation, and the lack of public support, many workers continued to secretly organize themselves into trade unions and openly press for better pay, better hours and better conditions.

By 1815, a number of textile mills were well established along the rivers of New England. These factories were ample evidence of America's ability to take care of her own needs without reliance on her friends abroad. But England, once again, had become an enemy.

Between 1807-1812, England seized American ships trading with France. The French and British were at war with each other. Also, England seized American sailors who were born in Great Britain. Although naturalized American citizens, the sailors were pressed into service for the British navy. Worse still, England blockaded American ports, cutting off supplies to the

17

United States from everywhere. Furious, America declared war on Great Britain. For two and a half years, England and the United States battled each other. In the end, England lost and signed a peace treaty on December 24, 1814.

Actually, sleepy New England, home of most of the victimized sailors, had opposed America's entry into a war with England, which Congress had declared on June 18, 1812. Only two days before, on June 16th, England had lifted the blockade. But news traveled slowly then. By the time Congress knew of the event, weeks later, it was too late.

Once America became involved in the war, however,

A NEW ENGLAND FACTORY TOWN

New England quickly became the country's manufacturing center. The Northeast had the most abundant supply of water power necessary to run the mills. The war gave an urgency to America's needs. And New England factories began to produce in quantity what skilled artisans working by hand and alone could not produce. Division of labor, now more refined, made it possible. And one did not require much training or skill to work the machines that made the products.

Much of that work was done by women, teenage farm girls, and young children—boys and girls six to ten years old. The teenage girls thought it was glamorous to work in a city factory. The pay was better than what they earned on a farm. Besides, the excitement of city life was inducement enough. The younger children were

introduced to factory work for a different reason. Their parents thought it wise to keep them out of mischief and productive at the same time. Since there were no compulsory education laws, it was easy to put them to work in factories.

More to the point, however, women who needed work—widows, spinsters and others—along with teenage girls and children, worked for half the wages paid to men. They were all cheap labor. Skilled men, on the other hand—trained and experienced craftsmen—began to find themselves with fewer orders. Their prospects looked so bleak that some of them gave up their own independent shops to work in the factories where their skills were only partially needed. Still, they were paid more than women, teenage girls, and children.

By the time the War of 1812 had ended, the American factory system was well established in the American scheme of things. The country's complete industrialization was only a matter of time. Much of it would be accomplished before the century would end.

Whatever the advantages offered to some New England factory workers, chiefly teenage girls in Lowell, Massachusetts—education, medical attention, clean housing, good food, and proper counseling—the unhappiness among the majority of those who worked in factories elsewhere persisted and grew. Strong and hopeful people, working in a new and promising country, labored mightily within dingy interiors without promise and with little reward. There, in the dim light of the noisy factory, their strength, independence and dignity slowly crumbled. Trade unions were too weak, unsuccessful, and illegal to soften the anguish over low pay, long hours, and an impoverished living standard.

Still, in 1825, undaunted by their own despair, unwearied by labor's frustrations, and uncowed by the threat to their safety, women tailors of New York City defied the courts and challenged the mighty. They organized themselves into a dues paying union. It was the first union of skilled women in America, if not in the rest of the world.

In that same year, 1825, the British Parliament made English trade unions legal. The government repealed all laws against trade unions and their members. It would be 17 more years before American courts would do the same thing.

STRIKING WOMEN

III. POLITICS AND PROGRESS: 1825-1865

John Quincy Adams had no sooner taken the oath of office as the sixth American president in March, 1825, than the young United States was jolted toward its industrial future.

The Industrial Revolution had been gathering momentum for twenty-five years, picking up speed after the War of 1812. But the jolt that hurtled the country into the second quarter of the 19th century came not from the organizing women tailors of New York but from English and American steam locomotives. The railroad became a fact of life.

The first railroad to use steam power to haul people and freight opened in Great Britain in 1825 and was called the Stockton and Darlington Railroad. And before the year would end, John Stevens of Hoboken, New Jersey, would build a locomotive and operate it on a circular track in his backyard. A new industry had been born. Ahead loomed thousands of new and different jobs for workers, from laborers to machinists, requiring new skills. These skills would be used not only to build the vast network of tracks that would one day cover the United States coast to coast, but to build the engines and cars that would roll over those tracks with surprising speed. Later, the railroads and the fuel they used, coal, would become central to the progress of the American labor movement.

Meanwhile, in 1827, a number of different Philadelphia craft unions established a common council to deal with their problems in a more unified way. The council was called the Mechanics Union of Trade Associations. Hopefully, the solid front of their organization would give them all the strength they lacked as individuals. It did not. Trade unionism was not quite that popular with the courts, the government, the business community, or most of the people. Trade unionism had no political power. And political power was the legal answer to illegal unionism.

The following year, 1828, the year the Baltimore & Ohio Railroad was begun, skilled laborers in Philadelphia founded the Workingman's Party, the world's first political party sponsored by labor. For the next six years, the party advocated a ten-hour workday for everyone, free land in the West for the poor, and an end to debtor's prison. These prisons were filthy places filled mostly with working people whose only "crime" was being unable to pay a debt of as little as $1.00 to some heartless creditor. There the debtor languished and rotted his life away unable to earn the money necessary to gain release. If he was lucky, an imprisoned debtor could be freed by friends or relatives. But his luck would be questionable if his release was at the hands of an unscrupulous employer desirous of cheap labor. Usually, the debtor would have little to say about his working future. He was indebted to his new employer who could easily return him to the prison and often did.

In addition, the Workingman's Party demanded free public education for every child and an end to child labor. "No liberty without knowledge," it told the public, "no democracy without education."

The Workingman's Party was pictured as the "great unwashed rabble" by business interests who stood the most to lose if such a political party became powerful. And it nearly did. Between 1828-1834, the Workingman's Party had spread to nearly every large city in the country. Moreover, it managed to have a number of its

VIOLENCE AGAINST THE WORKINGMAN'S PARTY

candidates for public office elected. None of these elections was smooth. Violence attended party members wherever and whenever they met. Bloody heads and broken bones were delivered by the hired toughs who were sent by local businessmen to do as much damage as possible to the working man. The business community—the haves—were not about to see the working community—the have nots—have anything. Still, the party persisted. It helped to elect Andrew Jackson, friend of the poor and downtrodden, the seventh President of the United States in 1828 and again in 1832.

The Workingman's Party faded soon after Jackson won his second term, however. Many in the party thought that with Jackson in the White House, a decent future was assured. But when Jackson used federal troops to crush a strike on the Chesapeake & Ohio Canal in January, 1834, many had second thoughts about their futures. No one had ever used federal troops to break up a strike. Disillusionment set in. The violence continued. Fear, too, had left its mark. By the end of 1834, the Workingman's Party had all but disappeared.

But the Workingman's Party created its own monument, a permanent reminder that its efforts were not in vain. Its tireless agitation resulted in the abolishment of debtors' prisons in America, and the institution of free, tax-supported public education for America's children.

Many of those who were active in labor's reforms now found themselves without a political base from which they could influence legislation on behalf of the working man. In New York City, for example, a number of labor's diehards formed the first national federation of labor unions, the National Trade Union. They challenged Congress to make the ten-hour work day the law of the land. Congress did not budge—not in 1834.

While the work-day issue was being hurled at Congress, other more politically shrewd unionists joined the Loco Foco Democrats of New York City. The Loco Focos were Democrats whose political ideas were not always agreeable to the party regulars—the Jacksonian Democrats. The name "Loco Foco" was actually a brand of matches used at the time. Once, when regular Jacksonian Democrats tried to break up a meeting of the radical wing of their own party by turning off the gas lights in the meeting room, the rival democrats lit their matches—their Loco Focos—and the meeting continued. From that event on, the radical wing of the Democratic Party was called Loco Foco while Jackson was in office.

Further north, in Lowell, Massachusetts, young factory girls unsuccessfully protested wage cuts in 1834 and 1836. They struck the mills by the thousands but to no avail. Outraged by their long hours, hard work and poor wages, they formed the Factory Girls Association and went back to their low paying, twelve-hour work day hoping for a better year.

Despite labor's seeming failures to achieve a better

life for working people, the federal government felt the pressure. During the thirty-year period beginning in 1806, the year union organizing and striking was declared illegal for an entire generation, the population of the United States grew from about six million to fifteen million people. This represented a growth of 150%, and it was chiefly among the working classes. That was the pressure. In 1836, the government budged a little. It ordered the Philadelphia Navy Yard to work a ten-hour day.

In 1840, President Martin Van Buren—once Jackson's Vice President—ordered a ten-hour work day for all federal employees. Now labor was becoming enough of a force to have the courts reexamine its right to organize and to strike.

Accordingly, in 1842, Chief Justice Lemuel Shaw of the Massachusetts Supreme Court handed down a landmark decision* favorable to labor. He ruled that it was perfectly legal for working people to organize unions and perfectly legal for unions to strike. They did. The business interests of New England, noted for their God-fearing piety but not necessarily for their generosity toward their fellow men and women in their employ, were understandably shaken, but they remained unworried.

By this time, many skilled workers were fleeing to

*Commonwealth of Massachusetts vs. Hunt.

farms and western lands, fed up with their industrial lot in the cities and towns. Over the next eighteen years, 1842-1860, the vacuum would be filled by a wave of Irish, German, and Scandinavian immigrants who would help swell the population to nearly thirty-two million. And immigrants would bend to the will of business, so thought businessmen.

But the pressure continued. Also, between 1842-1860, seven states* made the ten-hour work day law; the National Trade Union reorganized; and the shoemakers of Massachusetts, the first to organize themselves more than two hundred years before, staged the largest turnout as the Civil War (1861-1865) broke upon the nation. They struck for higher wages. Others struck, too. But the general feeling among American workers in the northern manufacturing centers was to preserve the Union—the union of states. Again, an uneasy truce was effected between workers and employers as the federal government went to war against the rebellious states of the South. Northern skilled labor, the heart of America's industrial strength, set aside its struggle temporarily and went to war, ready to take up labor's cause at the war's end. Most of these skilled workmen had little choice. They did not have the $300 necessary to buy their way out of military service, something wealthier businessmen were able to do.

---

*California, Connecticut, Georgia, Maine, New Hampshire, Pennsylvania, and Rhode Island.

AN 1860'S DEMONSTRATION

IV. TOWARD SURVIVAL: 1865-1900

One year following the end of the war, as the death of Abraham Lincoln was still being mourned everywhere, the first in a line of dynamic American labor leaders emerged. He was William H. Sylvis, a Pennsylvania ironworker. Sylvis had already organized the country's 9,000 iron molders into the strongest craft union yet seen. And with this strength he began demanding an eight-hour work day. He sought to weld the various labor groups—trade unions; blacks, who were excluded from union membership; and women, who had no voting rights at all—into one large labor organization. What he really wanted was a national political labor party that would rival the Democrats and Republicans and someday elect an American president from their ranks.

In 1866, Sylvis and others formed the National Labor Union on a platform of an eight-hour day and other reforms. Three hundred thousand of the nation's work force—organized, unorganized, disorganized—comprised the new amalgamation of workers. Within a few years its membership would double. Excluded from participation in the National Labor Union were black working people, a decision that Sylvis fought to prevent. The blacks formed their own national labor union, the National Colored Union, and enrolled white workers. Isaac Meyers, delivered from slavery only three

WILLIAM H. SYLVIS

years before, became its president, risking his life to organize southern blacks. Meyers was followed by the second and final president of the National Colored Union, Frederick Douglass.

Sylvis went on to become the National Labor Union's president in 1868. Congress seemed to react to Sylvis' growing power by ordering an eight-hour work day for federal employees. Connecticut and Illinois already had passed legislation enacting eight-hour work days. Pennsylvania responded with an eight-hour day in 1868, as did New York two years later. But most of these laws were only binding on employers if they and their employees had no prior work agreement. In other words, if a worker signed a contract to work ten hours a day in a state where the eight-hour work day was law, he had to work "as agreed." The law could not touch the employer or save the worker.

Sylvis did not live long enough to complete his mission. A year later, in 1869, he was dead at the age of forty-one. Without his leadership, a leadership that saw him die penniless having given his energy, his life, and his possessions to labor's cause, the National Labor Union began to founder.

As the NLU struggled to stay healthy, another great labor association was born, the Noble and Holy Order of the Knights of Labor.

Uriah S. Stephens, a Philadelphia tailor who once had notions about being a minister, dreamed of a "brotherhood" of working people. It would be an organization that would bind the skilled and the unskilled into a society to gain a greater share of the nation's wealth. His opportunity came late in 1869 when garment cutters in Philadelphia dissolved their bankrupt union. Then Stephens and eight former members of that union founded the Knights of Labor.

Stephens envisioned a worldwide society that would spiritually, as well as practically, lift the working people of this earth from "wage slavery." But Stephens would have a difficult time promoting his idea. From its inception, the Knights of Labor was a secret society that used various and complicated ceremonies, codes, symbols, prayers, and handshakes to create a spiritual aura

THE KNIGHTS OF LABOR INSIGNIA

about its mission, and to prevent anti-unionists from attacking them. The Knights of Labor wanted no one, especially employers, to know its true purpose. And so the Knights adopted the trappings and appearance of a fraternal order like the Elks.

In less than a year, the original nine members became fifteen. Soon their door would open a crack to admit others. The next several years would be a time of growth for the Knights of Labor.

In 1872, as the Knights began to establish a firmer grip on labor's pool of humanity, the late William H. Sylvis' National Labor Union had become the National Labor Reform Party, a seeming fulfillment of Sylvis' dream. The party offered United States Supreme Court Justice David Davis, a Lincoln appointee, as its presidential candidate in the election that would see the Republican incumbent, Ulysses S. Grant, win a second term. Grant's final opponent was Horace Greeley, famed editor of the New York *Tribune,* who ran as a Democrat and a Liberal Republican. Davis, however, withdrew from the race. His withdrawal caused the collapse of the National Labor Reform Party, bringing Sylvis' dream to an end.

Many labor activists were unsure about the effectiveness of a third party—a labor party—in the American two-party political system. Some of these believed that labor's problems should be solved legislatively through the two-party system. Others believed that their ends could only be achieved through non-political action—violence, if necessary. Also, there were some serious labor leaders whose only concern was not strikes, or violence, or work day hours, but the private ownership of land, the railroads and the telegraph. These things, they reasoned, belonged to the people and should be run by the government, not by individuals who stood to gain money and power at the expense of others.

Between 1873 and 1879, as Americans prepared to celebrate one hundred years of independence, a series of events took place that put much of the country on the edge of hysteria. The six-year episode of crises and terror was triggered by an economic depression following the Panic of 1873.

URIAH S. STEPHENS

In 1873, many of the nation's small banks failed after a large banking business headed by Jaye Cooke collapsed following disastrous investments. The panic that occurred touched off one business failure after another. The country lost confidence in itself; an enormous depression began; and people lost hope. Four million people were out of work, hungry, homeless, and desperate. The people took to the streets.

On a cold January morning in 1874, 50,000 wretched individuals met quietly in Tompkins Square, New York City, seeking an answer to their plight. As they waited patiently, the throng was charged by mounted police. Many were injured by the charging horses and police clubs. The roaring, frightened crowd fled in every direction, trampling beneath them the wives and children of others.

THE TOMPKINS SQUARE INCIDENT

Strikes broke out everywhere as employees protested wage cuts by employers who were trying to save their firms. The worst of these strikes midway through the depression took place in the Pennsylvania coal fields. There, Irish immigrant miners, poorly paid, poorly housed in company houses, in debt to the company store for food they could hardly afford, and in debt to the company itself for rent they could not pay, struck the coal fields. Their union, the Workingmen's Benevolent Association, became the target of the mine operators who reasoned that if they could destroy the union, they could break the strike.

Word was passed around everytime a mine manager was beaten that a secret organization of miners called "Molly Maguires" was responsible for these acts of violence. No one could prove this. No one was even sure that such an organization as the Molly Maguires existed. But the mine owners insisted that the Mollies were very real. Not only that, they were also convinced that the Molly Maguires, the Workingmen's Benevolent Association, and the Ancient Order of Hibernians, a social-charitable organization founded in 1836 to assist the needy Irish, all formed a great conspiracy of crime and terror. The mine owners employed strike-breaking detective Allan Pinkerton, former head of the United States Secret Service, to put down the strike. But Pinkerton's real job was to destroy the union.

Pinkerton had the union infiltrated by one of his Irish operatives, James McParlan. McParlan got nowhere until a striker, or several strikers—no one knew who or how many—shot and killed several foremen who represented the owners. The members of the union were just as shocked at the murders as were the mine owners. The union never sanctioned such crime.

McParlan arrested several alleged murderers. Evidence was furnished that the accused were Molly Maguires, union men, and members of the Ancient Order of Hibernians. Warrants were issued for the arrest of all the union leaders, who were charged with complicity in the crimes. Twenty-four miners went to trial in 1875.

They were all found guilty. Fourteen went to jail. Ten were hanged two years later. The country, now numbering some 45,000,000 people, less than one hundred thousand of whom actually belonged to a union, was generally unsympathetic.

The Pennsylvania coal field strike was over. The Workingmen's Benevolent Association was destroyed. The miners were forced back to work, having won nothing but more misery. An army of hired guns patrolled the mines, virtually imprisoning the miners, making sure they would never again raise their collective voices to protest anything.

But the trouble was far from over. The depression deepend. More businesses failed. More people lost their jobs. The ranks of the unemployed grew to alarming proportions. Those who managed to keep their jobs worked for such little pay that they might just as well have been unemployed. The unrest spread from city to city. The worst was yet to come.

On July 16, 1877, the Baltimore & Ohio Railroad cut the wages for all its workers. The cuts were so devastating that a working man putting in an eight-to ten-hour day could hardly support himself let alone his family. Outraged by the cuts which protected the profits of the millionaire railroad magnates, whose personal lives were not affected by the depression, railroad workers in Martinsburg, West Virginia, seized the line's properties. They tied up the railroad's services in and out of the town, offering to restore property and service when their wages were restored. Within days, strikes of railroad workers broke out everywhere. The nation's rail lines came to a halt. Nothing moved between New York and San Francisco.

President Rutherford B. Hayes ordered troops to Martinsburg. The troops were met by the strikers. Shots were fired. Strikers fell dead. Enraged townspeople destroyed the railroad's properties in a pitched battle with the soldiers.

More troops were sent to Pittsburgh. There they were met by more demonstrators. Again shots were fired. Twenty-six people died. Enraged further by the sight of American soldiers shooting at American citizens, more than 20,000 people attacked the 600 soldiers and drove them out of Pittsburgh, destroying much of the city in the process.

Americans in every major city—including New York, Boston, Chicago, Baltimore, St. Louis, and San Francisco—took to the streets to protest the greed of the railroad owners and the use of troops to protect the riches of those owners at the expense of the impoverished workers.

Pitched battles between troops, militia, police, and the poverty-stricken, demoralized working people—unemployed for the most part—now occurred everywhere. To many it seemed as if the country was in the midst of an armed rebellion.

The *New York Herald* called the rioters "wild beasts . . . to be shot down." At the same time a Pittsburgh grand jury called the use of troops and the shooting of strikers "murder." The Chicago *Daily News* blamed the railroad owners for the strike, saying that they had operated outside the law, "plundering the roads . . . to their own enrichment."

In many instances, soldiers and militiamen who came from the ranks of workers refused to shoot strikers. Still the shooting went on. Thousands were injured. One hundred or more died that July.

TROOPS IN PITTSBURGH

By August, the Railway Strike of 1877 was crushed. Some workers went back to work for a pittance. Others had some of their previous wages restored to a living level. Still others were fired for having struck in the first place. The railroad owners formed private armies to protect their empire of tracks and cars against any such future occurrences. State governments supported them by building armories in the major cities to house men and weapons in the event that troops would again be necessary to protect industry from the people.

While management girded itself for more labor unrest, business began to improve. The depression of the 1870's was nearing an end. A few voices could be heard in the business community saying that the labor force in America—the majority of citizens now numbering about fifty million—could not be dealt with harshly forever if business was to survive. As far as labor was concerned, it did not intend to be dealt with so harshly in the future.

In 1879, the leadership of the Knights of Labor passed from its mystical chieftain, Uriah S. Stephens, to Terence V. Powderly, a Pennsylvania mechanic. During the depression years, many unions and their branches, or "locals," went bankrupt and disappeared. Those that struggled on merged as the Federation of Organized Trades and Labor Unions of the United States and Canada. This conglomeration of loosely knit and weakened unions was short-lived (1881-1886). It proved to be no match for the Knights of Labor.

Soon after Powderly assumed leadership, he put an end to the "holy" and "noble" and "secret" ways of the Knights. He revised the name to the Order of the Knights of Labor and invited everyone to join, blacks and whites, and skilled and unskilled working people. Between 1879-1886, the Knights of Labor grew from an uncertain number—some historians put it at about 20,000—to more than 700,000. But events in 1886 would prove disastrous for the Federation of Organized Trades and Labor Unions in the United States and Canada, undermine the strength of the Order of the Knights of Labor from which it would never recover, and set back labor's cause once again.

TERENCE V. POWDERLY

The Federation of Organized Trades and Labor Unions voted for a nationwide strike to force business and government to recognize the eight-hour day. Powderly, who opposed strikes, appealed to the Knights to disassociate itself from the plan. Few members listened. Workers across the country readied themselves for the walkout.

Beginning Saturday, May 1, 1886 and continuing for the next several days, nearly a half million workers demonstrated all over the United States. The center of activity of the strike was in Chicago. There, a number of street corner orators, known to be anarchists, exhorted the largely peaceful crowds to overthrow the government of the United States. In their view the government had been unresponsive to the cries of the working poor. Among these orators was August Spies, the editor of a German-language radical newspaper.

THE HAYMARKET BOMBING

Spies called for a rally to protest the killing of a striker by police at the McCormick Harvester Company. On the evening of May 4, a small crowd assembled in Haymarket Square to listen to Spies and several others. Bored, the crowd which included the mayor of Chicago, began to walk off when Chicago police appeared and ordered an end to the meeting. Until that moment all was peaceful. The rally was breaking up. Suddenly, the damp night air was shattered by a bomb. The crowd stampeded. The police opened fire. Scores were wounded or injured. Seven died, including a policeman. The entire country was shamed and sickened by the incident.

Eight men were arrested, including Spies. None of them had thrown the bomb or even knew who had thrown it. Yet the eight were tried and found guilty. Spies and three others were hanged in November, 1887. One of the condemned men committed suicide. The three remaining defendants were sent to jail. All eight —the living and the dead—were later pardoned by the governor of Illinois, who said the trial was unfair. The bomb thrower, whoever he was, went free.

As a result of the Haymarket incident, most Americans became distrustful of labor leaders and unions. They saw themselves, the working force, caught between giants of power struggling to destroy each other and using workers—ordinary people—to gain that power. On one hand were the capitalists—the business interests, employers and managers—backed by the government, forcing people to work under conditions they could not control and for wages that enslaved them to a meager existence. On the other hand, they envisioned labor leaders as men who by the snap of their fingers could cause havoc in the country that could cost the workers their pitiful jobs, if not their lives.

The Federation of Organized Trades and Labor Unions, which instigated the national strike that led to the killings and hangings in Chicago, could not withstand the shock of a nation's horror. They disbanded. The Order of the Knights of Labor, which disapproved of the strike, nevertheless caught much of the nation's

THE HAYMARKET HANGING

wrath. Many of its members quit, never to return. From that time on, the Knights declined as the guiding light in the American labor movement. Its place would be taken by the American Federation of Labor founded in Columbus, Ohio, on December 8, 1886.

Labor's recognition would be slow in coming. More blood would be spilled over the next one hundred years to gain that recognition. Yet, there were signs of progress. Congress created a Bureau of Labor under the Department of the Interior in 1884. The Bureau offered reports on working conditions that were made public. Those who might not have known soon found out that textile workers in Massachusetts sometimes earned less than $150 a year from which they had to house and feed families of three, four, and five or more people. The Bureau began to take testimony that indicated clearly the helplessness of the average American worker, regardless of his or her trade.

On February 26, 1885, the government took a great step to prevent labor competition. The Congress forbade "contract labor." It made illegal the practice of American employers signing a contract with an individual—usually an immigrant—for services at wages lower than those received by an American worker. No longer could American wage earners be put out of work by an immigrant who agreed to do the same job for less pay in return for the payment of his passage across the ocean.

Immediately following the Haymarket bombing, cigarmaking members of the Knights of Labor contested the idea that they could not belong to their own union, Cigarmakers International Union, and the Knights at the same time. Significantly, the Cigarmakers International, which was founded in New York City in 1872 with about 130 members, now was one of the strongest unions in America with some 13,000 members. Its leader was Samuel Gompers. Gompers was one of the founders of the Federation of Organized Trades and

SAMUEL GOMPERS

Labor Unions. However, like Terence Powderly of the Knights, Gompers wished to achieve better working conditions, higher pay, and shorter hours, along with a good measure of social acceptance for American workers. And like Powderly, he wished to secure all this without violence—without turning the general public against trade unionism. Similar to Powderly, an Irishman who rose from the congestion of Irish laborers, miners, and craftsmen in eastern Pennsylvania, Gompers, a Jew, rose from the congestion of bewildered immigrants who had flooded the Lower East Side of New York. But unlike Powderly, Gompers believed in a national federation of unions of skilled workers only. Powderly, on the other hand, believed in a single national union of skilled and unskilled workers.

Powderly took the occasion of the Haymarket bombing to disassociate the Knights from any connection with the Federation of Organized Trades and Labor Unions. Also, he removed the threat to his power suggested by the cigarmakers by having Gompers and his group kicked out of the Knights.

Gompers and his cigarmakers, together with miners, ironworkers, steel workers, and carpenters representing 25 unions with a combined membership of 317,000 workers, met in Columbus and founded the A.F. of L.— the American Federation of Labor. Within a year their membership rose to more than a half million dues paying skilled workers. And unlike the failing Knights of Labor, a worker could belong to the A.F. of L. and still be a member of his own union. The A.F. of L. was a well-established affiliation of unions from the outset. It would become the most durable force and spokesman for labor the country would have for years to come.

The emergence of the American Federation of Labor sent a clear signal to business and government alike, namely, that labor would not be cowed into submission or beaten into oblivion, and that the American worker, loyal to his country and form of government, deserved and earned the right to have a decent standard of life. The A.F. of L. sent another signal to the unorganized worker that it meant what it said—that labor organized under its banner could be relied on.

Between 1888 and 1892, labor flexed its muscle and tested the political arena once again. The Union Labor Party and the United Labor Party were formed. They nominated candidates for the upcoming presidential election of 1888. The winner was Benjamin Harrison, a Republican. He had beaten the incumbent Democrat, President Grover Cleveland. But Gompers and his associates knew that winning or losing elections was not of primary importance to labor's march. Events, not elections, would shape the course of action taken by organized labor. There would still be more struggles ahead.

Early in 1892, officials of the Amalgamated Association of Iron and Steel Workers were told that the current wages of union members working in the Homestead mill of the Carnegie Steel Company, Pittsburgh, would be reduced. In addition, they were told that the company intended to cancel its work agreement with the union ahead of time. Andrew Carnegie, the multimillionaire founder of the company, who rose from the ranks of immigrant factory workers, had made a decision. He wanted immigrant nonunion labor. Immigrant nonunion labor worked for less money. The outraged union struck the company. Carnegie ordered his manager, Henry Clay Frick, to shut down the plant and fire everyone. He did, installing barbed wire and fences to "lock out" the union workers now jobless.

THE HOMESTEAD BATTLE

Frick then hired 300 armed Pinkerton detectives to break up the strikers and prevent anyone except non-union workers from entering the mill. The detectives were met at the mill's river landing by a force of armed strikers. Shooting broke out. Sixteen people died. More were wounded. By the end of that day, July 6, 1892, the Pinkertons surrendered. They were mauled by a mob as they were marched out of town.

Frick did not give up easily. When other steel mills in the area were struck by workers sympathetic to the plight of the locked-out Homestead steelworkers, he had the local sheriff ask the governor of Pennsylvania for National Guard troops. Along with the troops came a horde of nonunion strikebreakers who were admitted

to the mill under the protection of the soldiers. Frick then made another offer to the strikers: work under the conditions set by the company or starve. Most of the workers, union and some sympathetic nonunion, returned to the mill. The Homestead Steel Strike had ended. Labor lost, intimidated by armed force, humiliated by the work-or-starve standard set by big business.

There were other armed conflicts around the country that year between strikers and hired strikebreakers. One notable battle took place in Idaho at the Coeur d'Alene silver mine. There, too, as in other instances, federal troops were called out to restore order, often in favor of the company involved.

In June, 1894, two years after the Homestead Strike, the nation faced yet another ordeal, the Pullman Strike.

Chicago industrialist, George Mortimer Pullman, a one-time cabinetmaker, made his fortune by inventing sleeping cars for railroads—"Pullmans." The Pullman Palace Car Company had been manufacturing the cars since 1880 in a plant outside of Chicago. His workers lived in Pullman, a company-owned town. It appeared to be the most efficient and pleasant environment in America. There, to George Pullman's pride, his employees lived in company houses, shopped in company stores, attended company schools, worshipped in company churches, and in short had all of their needs cared for by the company—but none of it for free. But the appearance of paradise seen through the idealizing eyes

of the impressed visitor was belied by the fear that if
George Pullman ever decided to cut wages, no one
would be able to afford the goods and services in the
town of Pullman unless they were reduced accordingly.
If not, they, the workers, the inhabitants of Pullman,
would end up in debt to the company, bound to their
jobs to pay the debts—a form of servitude just short of
slavery. No one trusted Pullman's paternalism, his ef-
fort to appear to give his employees trouble-free lives.

In May, 1894, Pullman's employees realized their
worst fears. In order to make his cars more saleable,
Pullman reduced their purchase price. To make this

GEORGE M. PULLMAN

possible, he also reduced wages. When informed of the cut, a committee of workers asked Pullman to cut the rents and other costs in the town. He refused, telling them that one thing had nothing to do with the other.

EUGENE V. DEBS ORDERS RAILROAD STRIKE

In addition, the company refused to cut its dividends to shareholders.

Angered by Pullman's stand, 3,000 Pullman employees walked off their jobs on May 11th. The strikers received additional support from the 150,000 member American Railway Union headed by Eugene V. Debs. Debs would later found the American Socialist Party and become its candidate for president of the United States five times. Now, however, in June, 1894, his powerful railway union warned Pullman to reconsider or face a nationwide boycott. Pullman remained silent.

On June 26th, Debs ordered his union to disconnect all Pullman sleeping cars from trains everywhere in the country. They did. The rail lines refused to run their trains without the cars. Within days, hardly a train moved anywhere in the country. The United States, particularly in the West where Pullman cars were widely used, was almost paralyzed by the striking railway workers. The federal government quickly entered the dispute when the rail stoppage effectively halted the delivery of United States mail.

Under the terms of the recently enacted Sherman Antitrust Act of 1890, a federal law passed to prevent organizations from forming monopolies which could restrain trade and discourage competition, an injunction was issued to force the union to discontinue its strike, because it was restraining trade. The injunction, a court order requiring a person or persons or organization to stop an activity harmful to others until the courts decide whether or not the activity has merit and is legal, was backed by a show of force. President Grover Cleveland ordered 2,000 United States Army troops into Chicago where some violence had been reported. His purpose was to break a strike that was interfering with a function of the government—the free passage of the mails.

The appearance of the United States Army encampment on the shores of Lake Michigan ended the strike. Pullman had his way. The country moved again. Labor lost another contest. Eugene V. Debs was sent to jail for his part in the strike and charged with contempt of court for not obeying the injunction immediately. Nonetheless, on Monday, September 3, 1894, the entire

U.S. ARMY ENCAMPMENT IN CHICAGO

country celebrated its first official Labor Day, a national holiday signed into law by President Grover Cleveland to honor the American worker.

Before the century ended, a sign appeared to give everyone hope—business and labor alike—that an atmosphere of peaceful negotiation to solve labor-management disputes could prevail instead of armed conflict. On June 1, 1898, Congress passed the Erdman Act, a law designed to have a third party—in this case the government—to try to iron out disputes between labor and business to everyone's satisfaction. Under the law, the chairman of the Interstate Commerce Commission and the commissioner of the Bureau of Labor would mediate disputes between labor and business.

In time, labor and business would become more responsive to each other's needs. Collective bargaining —negotiation between organized workers and their employers—would become the acceptable method for resolving problems. Many leaders in both labor and industry would come to realize that what was at stake was not the survival of one at the expense of the other, but the survival of the United States as a productive nation providing a peaceful, decent, and secure standard of life for its people.

Index

National Colored Union, 30, 32
National Labor Reform Party, 34
National Labor Union, 30, 32, 34
National Trade Union, 26, 28

Panic of 1873, 35-37
Pinkerton, Allan, 38
Powderly, Terence V., 42, 43, 44, 50
Pullman, George M., 54-57
Pullman Strike, 54-58

Railway Strike of 1877, 42
Revolutionary War, 9

Shaw, Lemuel, 27
Sherman Antitrust Act, 57
societies, 9, 10
Spies, August, 44, 45, 46
Stephens, Uriah, S., 32, 35, 42
Stevens, John, 22

Stockton and Darlington Railroad, 22
strikes, 9, 10, 16, 17, 25, 26, 27, 28, 37,
    40, 41, 42, 44, 52-58
Sylvis, William H., 30, 31, 32

ten-hour workday, 10, 15, 26, 27, 28
Tompkins Square, 36

Union Labor Party, 51
United Labor Party, 51

Van Buren, Martin, 27

War of 1812, 18, 20, 22
Watt, James, 12
Whitney, Eli, 15
Workingmen's Benevolent Association,
    37, 38, 39
Workingman's Party, 23, 24, 25